To RITA,

"Lead Confidently!"

[signature]

Become a Better Leader in 30 Days

Steve Richardson

WestBow
PRESS
A DIVISION OF THOMAS NELSON

WestBow Press books may be ordered through booksellers or by contacting:

WestBow Press
A Division of Thomas Nelson
1663 Liberty Drive
Bloomington, IN 47403
www.westbowpress.com
1 (866) 928-1240

ISBN: 978-1-4908-1081-2 (sc)
ISBN: 978-1-4908-1082-9 (e)

Library of Congress Control Number: 2013918434

Printed in the United States of America.

WestBow Press rev. date: 10/18/2013

This book is dedicated to my wife, Stephanie, who has stood with me in all my leadership ups and downs. She has been my constant supporter and best friend. I would follow her anywhere.

Table of Contents

Introduction

Is it possible to be become a better leader in 30 days? Absolutely! Most of us have read one too many books on leadership. We have found them helpful and they have increased what I call our "leadership awareness." But the question is, "How much of what we read did we actually implement into our everyday leadership style and practice?"

It is the goal of this book to do just that! We have all heard that it takes about 30 days to change a habit. Well, my goal is to help you change your leadership perspective and hopefully some of your habits in 30 days. I don't expect you to embrace all the concepts and practices that are outlined, but if just one really hits home, you will become a better leader.

You will notice that I use both the words leader and manager throughout this book. Many authors find a sharp distinction between the two; I don't. I have a saying that I have used through the years which I'm certain isn't original with me: "All leaders manage, but not all managers lead." For me the two words are closely aligned, but not exactly the same. They differ in emphasis and how you relate to the people following you.

This book is designed to be read one chapter a day. Yes, I really mean that! There are many of you who could read this book in two hours, but that is not the point. Each chapter has an action item for you to complete. Don't worry, they're not hard! If you do them, they will help you change your leadership perspective, and yes, possibly your habits.

This book is also designed to be read in the order in which it was written. There is a thematic method that moves through the book. I know that many of you will see a chapter that looks interesting and that's what you'll want to read. That's okay! But, please keep in mind that many of the chapters build on one another.

I have been leading and managing people for over 30 years, and to the best of my ability, have employed everything you will read in this book. Being a leader is not for everyone, but we all find ourselves in leadership roles from time to time. When we do, we want to be the best leader we can be. Let me know if after 30 days you've become a better leader.

Well, now you have your instructions, so go for it!

Who's Following You?

I have a friend who was the president of a major company. He was addicted to reading the latest and greatest books on leadership, team building, hiring the right people, etc. I asked him one day what he had learned on how to spot the up and coming leaders in his company. His answer has stuck with me all these years. He said, "I finally decided to stop reading and to look and see who was following whom." His observation was so simple, yet so profound, "If no one is following you, you're not a leader."

When you were a kid, did you ever play a game called "follow the leader?" It is a very simple game; a group of children get together, pick a leader, and then follow him or her and do whatever he or she says or does. Usually everybody takes turns at being the leader. Over time an interesting thing happens among the circle of friends that consistently play the game. They usually end up wanting the same people to lead all the time. The followers choose the leader. Since this game is most popular between the ages of 6-8 we know that these kids have not studied leadership theory. What do they see in some of their friends that they do not see in others that makes them want to follow one more than another?

I played this game often when I was a kid. One of my favorite leaders was Mike. When he led it was never boring. He always came up with something new and he didn't do stupid things.

1

On the other hand, there was John. He really liked being the leader and tried to make us do things that were just scary and sometimes dangerous. Some would try to do what he asked, but most of us just said, "No!" Guess what happened? Mike got picked to lead all the time and John hardly ever got picked.

So, here is a basic leadership rule: Look behind you. If no one is following you, then you're not leading.

ACTIVITY FOR THE DAY

In all of your various settings today, look behind you and see if anyone is following you. Next, write their names down. Do this at work, home and any place else where you think someone is following you.

_____

_____

_____

_____

_____

_____

_____

_____

_____

_____

_____

_____

_____

_____

_____

_____

_____

_____

_____

Why Do People Follow You?

Remember yesterday's question you asked yourself about who was following you?

Perhaps the most important question that can be asked or answered is, "Why does anyone follow anyone?" Most of us would like to view ourselves as independent thinkers and action takers. We will listen to advice, but will make our own decisions, thank you very much! The sentiment for most of us is, "I don't really need other people telling me what to do, right?"

Do any of these statements sound familiar to you? As much as I would like to believe these statements, my experience has taught me something very different. I have learned that most people do not want to lead; they would much rather follow. There are many reasons for this attitude ranging from not caring to not wanting the responsibility that comes with leading. Also, many people are just afraid to be in charge.

Here is a basic truth to keep in mind: We have all followed someone at sometime.

Once you have looked behind you, two questions will emerge depending on what your observation is: "Why are they following me?" or "Why aren't they following me?" Today, I will try to answer these questions. The second question is the easier one to answer, so I will tackle it first. If people are not following you it is because: 1) they do not believe you know what you are doing, 2) they do not like you, or 3) they do not trust you. Most often it is a combination of all three. Here is what is interesting—If you do not know what you are doing people will not trust you, and if you are not very likable, people will not trust you. And, sometimes people will not trust you even when you know what you are doing and are likable. Do you see a pattern here? Yes, I think you do. It is the concept of trust. It is the key to why any of us will follow anyone.

We will discuss what makes people trust you on another day, but now on to that first question "Why are they following me?" If people are following you, are they doing it because they have to or want to? We have to follow leaders all the time that we would rather not follow. This happens most commonly at work, but sometimes in our social settings as well as at home. We do not have a choice at work because usually our paycheck depends on it. We have to do what the boss says. But then, there are people we follow because we want to whether it is at work, home, or in our social activities. They may not be our direct supervisor at work, but we look to them for advice and direction (something a leader dispenses to their followers). People will follow them because they have placed some level of trust in that leader. These are the types of followers all leaders want.

ACTIVITY FOR THE DAY

Take your list from day one and ask yourself this question: "Are they following me because they have to, or because they want to?" Put an "H" beside the names that have to follow and a "W" beside the names because they want to follow you. Here is some good news—people who *have* to follow you many times *want* to follow you! Put a big "HW" by their names.

_____

_____

_____

_____

_____

_____

_____

_____

_____

_____

_____

_____

_____

_____

_____

_____

_____

_____

What Does A Willing Follower Look Like?

So, what have you learned so far? One, to be a leader, there must be followers. Two, followers follow either because they have to or want to.

Today we want to discover what a willing follower looks like; how they react and behave toward the leader they are following. A willing follower engages in three actions that demonstrate trust in the leader they are following:

1) They will do what you ask them to DO
2) They will go where you GO
3) They will DEFEND you and your ideas to others

And here is the most important thing: they will do all three of these things WILLINGLY! You, as the leader, will not have to coerce or browbeat them into doing this. It does not mean that they will not question, argue or challenge you as the leader, but at the end of the day they will willingly DO, GO, and DEFEND you. These are all things that a trusting person will do. They do not do it blindly, but thoughtfully and willingly.

Let's test these three actions on ourselves. Think of someone that you willingly follow and ask yourself: "Would you do what they ask?" "Would you go where they go?"

"Would you defend them and their ideas to others?"

If your answer is "yes", then that person is a real leader in your life. Why? Because you have enough trust in them to follow them by DOING, GOING and DEFENDING.

ACTIVITY FOR THE DAY

Take the list you have been working on and look at every name that you placed a "W" beside and ask yourself this question, "Would that person willingly do what I ask, go where I go, and defend me and my ideas to others?"

Developing Trust: Charisma

So now you are ready to answer the question, "What makes a follower trust someone else to lead?" I think that there are three characteristics in a person that appeal to us in a way that allows us to extend trust to that person, and thereby be willing to follow that person as a leader. These characteristics can be summarized by three words: charisma, competence, and character.

We're going to tackle charisma first because it is the most difficult to define and it also has tremendous influence on how competence and character are perceived by others.

Charisma is very real, but subjective. It is somewhat mysterious and difficult to define, but easy to recognize. It's an emotional connection that makes you want to be around a person (to be in their sphere of influence). It is not a learned trait; you may naturally have a lot, some, or none. Think of people you just want to be around; they give energy to a room; people tend to revolve around them, like a magnet pulling everything to itself—that's charisma. I can assure you that all great leaders have strong charisma.

For those of you who would like a more technical definition, the English term charisma is from a Greek word meaning "favor freely given" or "gift of grace." The term and its plural are derived from the Greek word for "grace." Some derivatives from that root (including "grace") have similar meanings to the modern sense of personality charisma, such as "filled with attractiveness or charm", "kindness", "to bestow a favor or service", or "to be favored or blessed." The term has two main aspects: 1) compelling attractiveness or charm that can inspire devotion in others, and 2) a divinely conferred power or talent.

So, what does all this mean? Well, it certainly means that you cannot learn charisma in a classroom or by reading a book. It also means that if you don't have a decent amount of charisma in your personality, it will be much harder for you to engender trust from those who follow you; not impossible, but definitely harder.

I am certain by now that some of you are saying, "Holy Crap! Do I have any charisma?" To answer that question you need to ask yourself a couple of questions: "Do people gravitate to me in social and work settings?" And, "When I speak, do people tend to listen?" If your answers are "yes" to these two questions then you have some charisma.

Since charisma is a part of your personality force, it colors how people perceive you. Charisma encourages people to think positively of you, thereby opening the door to trust. Also, charisma can alter a person's perception of your competence and character. What do I mean by this? A person with strong charisma can be perceived to be more competent or possess more character than they really do. The follower can get caught up in the aura of the leader's charisma and no longer have an objective viewpoint of their competence or character. When this happens it can take a long time for the follower to gain a more objective view. This usually happens when the leader commits a grave act of character failure or gross incompetence.

So, it is not hard to understand why charisma is such a key element to developing trust.

ACTIVITY FOR THE DAY

Look around you for people you think have charisma. Write down their names. Observe how people interact with them; then ask yourself, "Do people interact with me that way?"

_____

_____

_____

_____

_____

_____

_____

_____

_____

_____

_____

_____

_____

_____

_____

_____

_____

_____

_____

Developing Trust: Competence

Let's face it, people like following people who know what they are doing! We want to believe that the person we are following is making good decisions and knows the subject matter in the area that we are following them.

Sounds simple, doesn't it. Well, it is simple if we are talking about the right competencies. There are two types of competencies: hard skills and soft skills. Hard skills are those skills that bring some sort of technical expertise to the table; such as accounting, legal, engineering, or medical skills. Soft skills are more intangible; such as problem-solving, decision-making, communication, etc.

For people to trust you, it is the soft skills that must be cultivated. People appreciate people with hard skills, but they will seldom follow them if they do not also have the necessary soft skills. I am sure that you have heard stories about a superb accountant, doctor or engineer who was promoted into a position of leadership because of their hard skills and then had to employ soft skills to lead their organizations. What do you think happened? Well, many of these cases ended up with a total failure in leadership, and we now know what that means—nobody was following them! These individuals were no longer able to engage their hard skills alone, which had earned them the position, and lacked the necessary soft skills needed to lead. This is a classic case of the Peter Principle that states that successful people are often promoted until they reach a position of incompetence.

Everyone who writes on leadership seems to have a different list of what the most critical soft skills are, but there are some that show up on most lists. Here they are: decision-making, strategic-thinking, problem-solving, and envisioning/motivating. We will tackle these soft skills later in this book.

Now, here is a very important thing to remember. There is a danger when looking at these three traits to overrate competence. It is necessary, but it is the least powerful in developing trust. Why do I say that? Because charisma and character color how our competencies are perceived. You can have good competencies, but the perception of them can be skewed through your charisma or character and they can be viewed negatively. Also, keep in mind that the opposite is true. Weaker competencies can be viewed more positively than they are because of your charisma or character. It takes all three working in harmony to become a great leader.

ACTIVITY FOR THE DAY

Write down the hard skills and soft skills that you believe you have today. Which list has the most? Now ask yourself, "Do I have the soft skills I need to build trust from others?"

_____

_____

_____

_____

_____

_____

_____

_____

_____

_____

_____

_____

_____

_____

_____

_____

_____

_____

_____

_____

Developing Trust: Character

Character can be defined in many ways, but when it comes to trust there are two character traits that stand out above the others. They are truthfulness and tenacity. If people believe you are truthful and tenacious they will tend to trust you enough to follow you.

I am certain that the first trait does not surprise you. We want our leaders to be truthful. This character trait is ingrained in American culture. We see it in two of our most highly esteemed presidents; George Washington and Abraham Lincoln. Remember the story about George Washington? As a boy he chopped down a cherry tree. When his father asked what happened to the tree, George replied, "I cannot tell a lie, I chopped down the cherry tree." I know the story is probably myth, but it conveys a principle that Washington was considered to be truthful.

The same can also be said for the moniker that has been ascribed to Abraham Lincoln, "Honest Abe." Lincoln, through his truthfulness and tenacity, developed trust among his followers to such an extent that the adjective "honest" became synonymous with his name.

It bears repeating, we want our leaders to be truthful with us. If that is the case, what do you think happens when we lie to the people who are following us, or if they begin to think we are holding the truth of a situation from them? It is not hard to imagine, is it? They will stop trusting us, and quit following us. There is probably no greater destructive force to trust than lying to those who follow you.

Is telling the truth to those who follow you always easy? Absolutely NOT! But, it is always better than lying to your followers.

Now, let's consider a trait that you are probably not as familiar with—tenacity.

Tenacity is a dogged persistence seeking a goal that is highly valued or desired. I like the mental picture of a small, feisty bulldog that has attached himself to your pant leg and no matter how hard you try to shake him off, he will not let go. We all want to follow a leader who will get us to the goal regardless of the obstacles along the way. There is a spirit of determination associated with this trait that inspires trust in us.

Two of my favorite historical examples are battlefield generals from American history: Ulysses S. Grant and George S. Patton. Both generals had testy social skills and questionable personal habits, but one thing was very clear from first-hand accounts of those who followed them: they would follow these generals anywhere, because they believed (trusted) these leaders would get them to the goal or victory. And, these two generals did not disappoint. They overcame a myriad of obstacles, resistance and setbacks to reach their goals.

People will follow you because they trust that you will get them to the goal, no matter what!

When these two traits of truth and tenacity mesh together, they create a powerful environment for trust.

Character also allows us as leaders to survive failure. We usually fail because of one of our incompetencies; poor decision-making, poor problem-solving, etc. But being truthful and tenacious allows our followers to "give us a break." Why? Because they believe our character will overcome our weaknesses.

ACTIVITY FOR THE DAY

Identify three people that you know who are truthful and tenacious. Do you trust them? Would you follow them?

_____

_____

_____

_____

_____

_____

_____

_____

_____

_____

_____

_____

_____

_____

_____

_____

_____

_____

_____

_____

_____

Walking On Water

I know—it's a weird title. However, it conveys a truth about what a great leader can ask of a follower. Are you curious?

There is a story from the Bible about Jesus and his disciples. Obviously, Jesus was a leader because people followed him; in particular a smaller group of disciples (followers) went everywhere with him.

The story goes that one evening after a long day Jesus sends his disciples ahead of him in a small boat to cross the lake. While they are making their way across the lake, the wind comes up and makes their sailing difficult. As they are struggling to maintain course and make shore, one of the disciples named Peter sees Jesus approaching the boat walking on the water. Well, they thought they were hallucinating or seeing a ghost. Peter decides to yell out, "Jesus, if that is really you, tell me to come out to you." The story continues with Jesus saying to Peter, "Come." So Peter hops out of the boat and heads toward Jesus, walking on the water until he looks down, becomes frightened and begins to sink. Jesus reaches his hand out to Peter and rescues him from sinking and says, "Why did you quit trusting?"

I've always found this to be a fascinating story because it raises a great leadership question. "Is there anyone I would be willing to try and walk on water for if they asked me?" Think of the level of trust it would take on the part of the follower to attempt what would appear to be impossible.

Here's the thing—A truly great leader (one who has strong charisma, character, and competence all working in harmony) can ask a follower to attempt the impossible (at least it seems impossible to the follower) and the follower will do it. It is this type of leadership that achieves great things because it empowers followers to attempt great things.

ACTIVITY FOR THE DAY

Is there anyone that you would be willing to do the impossible for if they asked you?

Would anyone try walking on water if you asked them?

_____

_____

_____

_____

_____

_____

_____

_____

_____

_____

_____

_____

_____

_____

_____

_____

_____

_____

Two Things People Want From A Leader: Part One

I have sat down with many followers through the years and asked them what they want from their leaders. They listed a variety of things; some we have already addressed in our first seven days. But there are two action words that continually pop up on the list of what followers want from their leaders. Here they are:

BE DIRECT

BE DECISIVE

The number one complaint that I have received from followers who were not happy with their leaders was that they were not being direct. The majority of followers do not like vagueness. They want to know exactly what a leader wants from them. They want to know how a leader feels and exactly why they are doing whatever it is they are supposed to be doing. You would be amazed at how many people in leadership are not direct.

So here is a key principle: It is always better to be too direct rather than to be vague. I do not know how many times I have heard from followers "If he/she would just tell me what they want, I would do it" or "If they didn't like it, why didn't they tell me?"

This raises a question, "If being direct is an important action in leadership, then why do so many leaders not do it?" Let me give you a couple of reasons. The first reason is connected to self-esteem. If I am overly concerned with what people will think of me, then I will tend to be less direct. Why? Because being direct will solicit a direct response, whereas being vague solicits a vague response. If I am afraid that someone will not like me if I am direct, I will feel more secure by being vague. The second reason for not being direct is connected to blame. If I am direct, then a follower can say, "You told me to do that," and thus the leader becomes responsible for the action. If I am indirect and unclear it is harder to blame me later.

These reasons have a common thread; they both reveal a leader who is more concerned about himself or herself than about their followers. When a follower senses that, their trust will begin to erode.

Do not underestimate the willingness of followers to accept directness from you as a leader. If you want something done, state it clearly. If you like or do not like something, say it. If you have a goal or plan, tell your followers clearly (and I would also add concisely!) Remember, if they trust you, they will go where you go and do what you say. But, that is hard to do if they are not certain where you are going or clearly understand what you said! So, be direct!

ACTIVITY FOR THE DAY

Ask three of your followers this question, "How direct do you think I am?" The answer may surprise you!

_____

_____

_____

_____

_____

_____

_____

_____

_____

_____

_____

_____

_____

_____

_____

_____

_____

_____

_____

Two Things People Want From A Leader: Part Two

Today we will discuss the second thing that followers want from their leaders—decisiveness.

Followers have an expectation that their leaders will make decisions. This is so basic that it seems silly to have to put it in print. Decision-making is the one action that all followers expect from their leaders. However, the sad reality is that many leaders avoid decision-making at all costs! You would be amazed at how many times I have heard a follower say, "If only they would make a decision" or "Why can't they just make a decision?"

This reminds me of a common discussion that happens every day in the workplace, socially and at home. It revolves around eating. The conversation usually goes like this,

"What do you feel like eating?"
"I don't know, what sounds good to you?"
"I don't care, whatever sounds good to you."
"What type food sounds good to you?"
"I don't know, how about you?"

This conversation can go on for quite awhile until someone finally says, "JUST MAKE A DECISION!" So here is another key principle: Followers usually do not care what decision you make as long as you make one. Can that really be true? Yes, it is.

Followers do not keep tabs on how many good or bad decisions you make, but they do remember if you are decisive. As a leader, we all make wrong decisions. We just need the majority of our decisions to be good ones or else we won't be able to lead our followers where we said we would take them.

Followers are very forgiving of poor decisions, especially if we are direct about it, and then make a good decision to put us back on the right track. In keeping with our illustration, most of the time it does not matter if it's Italian, Chinese, Mexican or American; just decide on one. Everyone is relieved and happy that a decision was made.

The same is true in our leadership role. When we worry about making the wrong decision, it can keep us from making any decision. No leader can afford to be indecisive and expect their followers to keep following.

One last thought—being direct and decisive demands a level of self-confidence as opposed to self-worry. You cannot think too much about what others will think of your directness or decisiveness. Much like the Nike ad—just do it!

ACTIVITY FOR THE DAY

Write down three decisions you made as a leader today. How did your followers react to them?

_____

_____

_____

_____

_____

_____

_____

_____

_____

_____

_____

_____

_____

_____

_____

_____

_____

_____

_____

_____

Taking Responsibility

Today we shift from looking at leadership from a follower's perspective to that of a leader's perspective.

Much of what we have talked about in the last two days can be summed up in the phrase "taking responsibility." When we are direct and decisive we are taking responsibility not only for what we say and decide, but also for what our followers will do with what we said and decided.

This is what some have called "the burden of leadership." At times it can weigh you down. Most leaders, at one time or another, get tired of being the one that is ultimately responsible. But, at the same time, readily recognize and agree with the old saying, "The buck stops here."

It is one of the reasons people will follow us. Most people do not want to be the one who is ultimately responsible. Most of us want someone else to do that, and for good reason—it's draining. Look at photos of recent American presidents before they took office and then at the end of their first term. You can see them literally age before your eyes. Leadership has a cost—responsibility.

So, what makes anyone want to take on the responsibility that comes with leadership? It never goes away; it tires you out; you get the blame or praise for things you did or did not do or that others did or did not do on your behalf.

I wish I had a "one size fits all" answer. There are certain words that come to mind when I try to answer this question for myself—ego, desire, vision. For me, as a leader, these words help express why I am willing to take on the responsibility. My ego feels rewarded; I have a desire to help people reach a goal; I truly believe that the vision of where I am leading people is worthwhile. These three words all mesh together for me in a way that is difficult to define. There may be different words for you.

One final thought on responsibility; it is strongly tied to a character trait that we discussed earlier—tenacity. The determination to get to where we promised our followers we would take them enables us to bear the responsibility that comes with that promise.

ACTIVITY FOR THE DAY

Write down three or four words that help you understand why you are willing to bear the responsibility of being a leader. Then put those words into sentences that will encourage you in "taking responsibility."

_____

_____

_____

_____

_____

_____

_____

_____

_____

_____

_____

_____

_____

_____

_____

_____

_____

_____

31

Your New Best Friends: Risk And Failure

These two words go hand in hand and every leader has to embrace them. I am always tempted to put people into two categories: risk-takers and risk-avoiders. I know that is an over simplification of why and how people behave, but it does help me quickly spot people who will slow me down or jump on board with me.

Let's talk about risk first. What is risk? What does it mean to us as leaders? Let's start with a definition:

> "Risk is the potential that a chosen action or activity (including the choice of inaction) will lead to a loss (an undesirable outcome)."

All actions or decisions carry a level of risk, therefore every action carries the possibility of failure. To be an effective leader you must learn how to measure risk, not how to avoid it. The truth is that you cannot avoid risk. You can decrease or increase it, but it is still there. Once you accept this fact, you can begin to look at risk differently. Followers expect their leaders to take risks, but followers also expect that their leaders will not lead them over a cliff!

So, the question for the day is, "How do we measure risk?" Here are some things I ask myself to measure risk:

1) Will the action have more likelihood of success vs. failure? (Sometimes I make a list of the pros and cons).
2) Will the action use up resources I can replace? If I cannot replace the resource (for example money) then the risk is far greater.
3) Will I be able to get my followers to embrace the risk with me?

After I go through these questions, I make a decision. I don't look back. Why? Because I believe I will succeed more often than I fail. My followers will accept the failures along the way because they know I am leading them forward and they trust me.

Now, let's talk about failure for a moment. Here is a universal truth: EVERYBODY FAILS. There are no exceptions. An effective leader learns how to accept failure and move on. One of the great myths you can tell yourself is "I am the leader, I cannot fail or people will not follow me."

One of my favorite illustrations about success and failure comes from baseball. Hitting is a major part of being a successful baseball player. One of the most successful baseball hitters to play the game was Ted Williams. He was the last player to bat over .400 in a single season. That was in 1941. He is number 7 on the all-time batting average list at .344. A name that most of us know, Babe Ruth is number 10 on the all-time batting average list at .342. Ty Cobb is number one at .366. The best hitters to ever play the game only succeeded in getting a hit 35% of the time. Ted Williams had one season where he succeeded 40% of the time. That means that 60%

or 65% of the time he didn't get a hit—he failed. Were these great hitters, who failed so often, still successful? YES! They measured the risk and knew that one out of three times they would be successful. In baseball, that is remarkable! You don't have to bat 1.000 to be successful.

Once we change our mindset about risk and failure, it will enable us to measure risk and deal with failure better.

ACTIVITY FOR THE DAY

For your next major decision, measure the risk. Make a list of the advantages and disadvantages, then make a decision and don't look back!

_____

_____

_____

_____

_____

_____

_____

_____

_____

_____

_____

_____

_____

_____

_____

_____

_____

_____

Don't Live With Mistakes

Yesterday we talked about risk and failure. We want to learn to measure risk and to accept that failure is part of leading. So what about mistakes? Are they different from failure? The answer is yes and no. If I add up a column of numbers wrong, that is a mistake. Did I fail to add properly?—Yes, but it is a failure that can be easily corrected. For me, mistakes are small failures that slow us down if we do not correct them. The type of failure we talked about yesterday is the risk of attempting something big and, at the end of the day, to have it fail.

So here is one of my leadership axioms: "If you live with a series of mistakes, they can lead to major failure, even if the risk was acceptable." Thus our title today—don't live with mistakes!

Followers do not want us to live with our mistakes either. The longer we wait to correct our mistakes, the more problems it causes our followers. What are some examples of mistakes we should not live with as leaders? Here are two recurring mistakes I have made through the years that can really slow you down if you do not address them in a timely manner.

1) Hiring the wrong people
2) Staying with an ineffective strategy too long

You cannot lead an organization or business without running into these two potential areas of wrong decision-making.

As a leader I hate hiring the wrong person or enacting an ineffective strategy. I always say to myself, "You should have known better." Every time I do it, it slows down the progress in achieving the big goal. But, I have hired the wrong person more than once and enacted strategies that didn't work many times. Will I keep hiring the wrong people and implementing ineffective strategies?—Probably. But, as I learn from my mistakes, I make them less often. It is much like our baseball illustration from yesterday—It's impossible to bat a thousand percent. So, knowing that . . . DON'T LIVE WITH MISTAKES!

How long is too long to live with a mistake? If some of your trusted followers start saying to you, "When are you going to do something about so and so?" or "You do know that this is not working?" it is too long. At that point you must act. My guess is that if your followers are talking to you about the mistake, you already knew you should have acted—their comments are just a confirmation.

As leaders we want to believe that all of our decisions are good ones, but we know that is not true. So, don't live with mistakes—your followers will thank you.

ACTIVITY FOR THE DAY

Write down two mistakes that you are living with. Come up with a plan to address and correct them soon!

_____

_____

_____

_____

_____

_____

_____

_____

_____

_____

_____

_____

_____

_____

_____

_____

_____

_____

_____

_____

_____

Never Underestimate Intuition

I believe everyone has intuition; some have more highly developed intuition than others. It is a necessary trait that leaders need to exercise.

Let's start with a definition that I like:

> "Intuition is a combination of historical (empirical) data, deep and heightened observation, and an ability to cut through the thickness of surface reality. Intuition is like a slow motion machine that captures data instantaneously and hits you like a ton of bricks. Intuition is a knowing, a sensing that is beyond the conscious understanding—a gut feeling."
>
> —Abella Arthur

Perhaps you have heard the saying, "trust your gut." It's just another way of saying, "use your intuition." Sometimes this is hard to do. Most of us are taught to trust what we can see or touch. Intuition connects things that we cannot see or touch. For that reason many of us are uncomfortable with trusting and using our intuition.

Are intuitive decisions always right? Of course not, but they can be as accurate as decisions that arise from our physical senses and data analysis. As leaders, we may be presented with several good options. But which one is best? We may run the numbers; add up the pros and cons and still not know. So what makes us ultimately choose one over the other? I believe it is intuition. Intuition connects the dots that we can't physically observe; it makes connections that we are unable to articulate. It means that our brains are amazing and can operate on a level that can connect our experience and knowledge in a way that we can't rationally think through.

How can we improve our intuition? First and foremost, accept that it is an important decision making tool. Second, start practicing. The easiest way to do this is to ask, "What is my gut reaction to this idea?" You will discover that you have intuitive responses to many things that require a decision. Next, go through your normal decision making process and see how your gut reaction lines up with your process. You'll find that they agree more times than not. As you become more comfortable with using your intuition, you will then have a greater tendency to trust it for making decisions.

ACTIVITY FOR THE DAY

Test your intuition (your gut reaction) on all of your decisions today. The best way to do this is to write down your gut reaction and test it against any data analysis you are using in your decision-making.

How's Your Vision?

People use many words to talk about where a leader is leading them: vision; goals; direction; mission. For most people who write about leadership this whole concept of vision is usually high on the list. I understand why; it speaks to where a leader is taking their followers. However, I think we make too much of the concept. Vision is not something you just make up. It reflects on who you are as a leader. The vision has to come from somewhere inside you that is deeply connected with your passion and values. It doesn't have to be life-changing; it doesn't have to be bigger than life.

Just how much vision do you need as a leader?

You need enough to get you where you want to go and enough to see farther ahead than your followers. It also needs to be big enough to motivate and interest your followers. It needs to be reachable, understandable, and motivating.

I think we get caught up in thinking of vision as some big, cosmos-changing thing. Most of what we read about vision only notes the big examples that change the course of history; Martin Luther King's vision of equality for all; John F. Kennedy's vision for putting a man on the moon, or Abraham Lincoln's vision for a slave-free country. Vision needs to fit the context of who and where we are as leaders. The examples cited above were all leaders on a national stage, which contextually called for a larger vision.

Let's look at a smaller context; one that represents many of us in leadership. Consider the small business owner. Their product may be donuts, gasoline, massages, construction, or light manufacturing. What does vision look like to them? What do they want for themselves, for their company and for their employees?

These questions all merge together into a direction, goal or vision. It could look something like this, "I have a vision to build a successful business (a brand that will be well respected regionally) that will provide financial security for my family and employees." This is a vision that fits the context of the leader, just as the big visions cited above fit the context of those leaders.

Let me give you a simple definition of a visionary. A visionary is a person with a clear, distinctive, and specific vision of the future. Guess what? We can all be visionaries.

Let me share one last thought on vision. Effective vision must answer two questions, "Where are we going?" and "Why are we going there?" I have a saying that expresses how these two questions blend together. "Vision is doing something that does something more." Let me give you an illustration. I want to build flying cars. That's where I want to go. Why? So that people no longer have to waste hours of their lives sitting in freeway traffic. Do you think I could get some followers to buy into that vision? They may have some questions about whether I could build the flying car, but the "why" is very motivating— everyone hates sitting in traffic!

ACTIVITY FOR THE DAY

Write down your personal vision. Write down your vision for your company or job (whatever your context is). Now merge the two visions together. Make certain you say where you're going and why. You are on your way to becoming a visionary!

_____

_____

_____

_____

_____

_____

_____

_____

_____

_____

_____

_____

_____

_____

_____

_____

_____

_____

_____

The Forest And The Trees

There is a proverbial saying that goes like this, "You cannot see the forest for the trees." What does it mean?

Have you ever taken a walk in the woods or been lucky enough to wander through redwood groves? If you have, then you saw the texture of the bark on the trees and the shape of the leaves. You probably noticed the built up layers of dead leaves, the ferns that thrive in the shade and quickly became aware that you had no idea how big the forest actually was.

Let's shift our perspective; you are now flying and as you look out the window you see miles of forest. The trees merge together and form an expansive canopy of various shades of green. You can see the boundaries of the forest; where they stop against the rising mountains or thin out as they approach the more arid regions. You cannot see the forest floor or the ferns that grow beneath that canopy.

Yesterday, we talked about vision. Vision is the forest. When you're in and among the trees, those are the details. For leaders the meaning is clear: DON'T LET YOUR VISION GET BOGGED DOWN IN THE DETAILS!

Why? Because you will get lost! If you lose your way, what do you think will happen to your followers? Your immediate response is probably, "But I cannot ignore the details or we won't reach our goal." My answer is, "You can visit the trees in the forest, but you can't stay there!"

As a leader, you must let your followers deal with the details. That doesn't mean that there are not some details that will demand your attention. But it is up to you to discern when to do that.

How does the forest and the trees metaphor apply to your followers? Well, if you are watching the forest, then they are tending the trees. And, if they are tending the trees, it is very easy for them to lose sight of the big picture. This is why, as leaders, we must consistently remind our followers of where we are going and why we are going there. Never miss an opportunity to remind them that the forest is far bigger than the trees they are walking through. So, you can see why it is so important for you to not get lost in the details. If you get lost, everyone will be lost!

ACTIVITY FOR THE DAY

What details do you need to let go of today that hinder your vision? Write them down.

_____

_____

_____

_____

_____

_____

_____

_____

_____

_____

_____

_____

_____

_____

_____

_____

_____

_____

_____

_____

Whoever Said Delegating Was Easy?

We have learned as a leader that you cannot get bogged down in the details. This means that you must delegate tasks to your followers so that you can reach your goal. This is much easier said than done! Most of us think that if I do it myself it will be done the way I want it, and on time because I won't have to explain how to do it to anyone. I will have no one to blame but myself. That may sound good, but it is all wrong from a leadership perspective. As leaders, we want to motivate and empower our followers. Delegating is one of the key ways we do this.

When I first mention delegating in a group of new leaders, they get very excited. I hear some of them say, "Great, I can give that crap I hate doing to someone else!" Wrong answer, but I bet you have had that thought cross your mind too. I hear others say, "I don't know if anything will be done right." Let me tell you—anyone who delegates has had that thought cross their mind.

So, to lead effectively you must delegate, but how do we do it effectively? Let me list some delegating principles we need to keep in mind:

People don't have to do it your way for it to be done well

I know this is hard for some of you to believe, but it's true. Several different paths can lead to the same place; so it is with delegating. Clearly communicate the task and the goal, and then let your follower run with it. By allowing flexibility in how the task can be done you can inspire creativity and greater productivity for the follower.

Other people may do it better than you

The fact is, as a leader, you should want other people to do many things better than you! Leaders should be gathering talented followers around them that bring various skills to help accomplish the vision. Do not be afraid of talented people doing something better than you; be happy, be very happy!

Delegate to people's strengths, not their weaknesses

I will talk more on this later, but for now understand that you will accomplish much more when you take the time to delegate to a follower's strength. They will be happier and much more productive.

Explain how it fits into the vision of where we are going

Followers like to feel that whatever task or project they are doing on behalf of the leader fits into the greater vision/goal. Take time to explain how a report or sales trip helps to reach your vision/goal.

Do not just delegate the "crap" you don't want to do (nobody enjoys the "crap" assignments)

I have delegated lots of tasks that my followers thought were "crap" assignments, but I also make it a point to give them good assignments; tasks that match their strengths and ones that they know are important to reaching our goal. There are always tasks that none of us are excited about doing, so spread them around, but do the same with meaningful tasks as well.

Do not just delegate the things you don't know, but the things you do know

Here is one of the pitfalls for many leaders. They easily hand off things they don't know and keep the things they do know. Part of being an effective leader is to know when to hand off the stuff you do know. Too often, we don't hand off the stuff we know, because we don't think we need to. But, we do need to delegate the stuff we know for several reasons: 1) it allows us to mentor our follower as they do the task, 2) it begins to build followers who can do what we do, and 3) it creates increased trust and confidence for the follower because they know you could have done this task yourself.

ACTIVITY FOR THE DAY

The Delegation Quiz:

Do I delegate as much as I should?	YES NO
Do I believe others can do it better than me?	YES NO
Do I just delegate "crap"?	YES NO
Do I delegate to people's strengths?	YES NO
Do I delegate the things I know?	YES NO

_____

_____

_____

_____

_____

_____

_____

_____

_____

_____

_____

_____

_____

_____

_____

Build On Strengths; Forget The Weaknesses

How many of us have gone through an interview where one of the questions was, "Please name your strengths and weaknesses?" Most of us rattle off a couple of strengths and then struggle to come up with a weakness that will still get us the job. Personally, I think this is one the dumbest interview questions that can be asked. I like this question much better, "What strengths do you see yourself bringing to our organization that would help us?" Do you see and feel the difference between those two questions?

Several years ago the Gallup organization developed a character trait tool called "Strength Finder." It became very popular and continues to have broad use. The concept was simple; help people discover themes that are areas of strength and encourage them to reflect on the identified strengths and incorporate them into their daily activities. When this tool came out, I thought it was great. It validated a little saying I had been using for some time as I led people in various settings, "Build on islands of strength and ignore the weaknesses."

There is a tendency to become too focused on a person's weaknesses instead of their strengths. We tend to do this in the annual review process in business. There seems to be a belief that we need to improve the weaknesses in our followers/

employees for them to be more effective. I believe just the opposite is true. We need to focus on a person's strengths and then find a way to best utilize them. As leaders, if we do this, we will have happy, productive and successful followers / employees.

We waste a lot of time trying to get people to strengthen their weaknesses, but much of the time to little avail. If I focus on people's strengths, I find that their weaknesses are not a hindrance. The one exception to this viewpoint is when a particular weakness begins to negatively impact a strength.

Let me give you an example:

I have an employee or follower that is great at building relationships and structuring business deals. This is their strength. To build relationships and structure business deals requires scheduling a lot of meetings. However, my employee/follower is constantly late to those meetings. This is their weakness. How long do you think they can keep showing up late to meetings before it begins to negatively impact their strength at building relationships? This is where a leader needs to step in and help the employee/follower understand how their strength is being negatively affected by a weakness.

Here are some action steps to help you be a leader that focuses of strengths:

1) Identify the strengths in your followers
2) Make certain you have them using their strengths
3) Do not focus on the weaknesses
4) Step in and give direction/correction when a weakness begins to hinder a strength

My grandfather owned a barber shop for most of his life. He had many sayings to convey a point to his customers. One that I remember that fits our topic today is "you catch more flies with honey than you do with vinegar." I believe that our followers will be more productive and happier if we praise them and use their strengths rather than constantly critiquing their weaknesses. Building on people's strengths will build success, which in turn will breed more success.

ACTIVITY FOR THE DAY

Pick three of your followers today. List their strengths. Are you using their strengths?

Leading And Teamwork

Teamwork is a word that has been overused and ill-defined over much of the last 20 years. We have been led to believe that teamwork is really a collegiate way of brainstorming, idea development and decision-making. I am here to tell you that most leaders I know would never look at teamwork that way—I certainly don't!

Let us look at sports for a moment, where the concept of teamwork really comes from. Let's take my favorite sport again, baseball. All baseball teams have a manager. What is his job? The manager selects who will play what position, what the batting order will be, who will pitch, and he makes calls during the game that will affect its outcome. If anyone is going to argue with the umpire, it should be him. If someone is benched, he does it. If someone is traded, he has a major say in that decision.

Now, do you think the manager has a team meeting to ask the players who should be playing second, or should be batting fourth? Of course not, he is the manager/leader and is expected to make those decisions even if the team doesn't like it. So then, where does the teamwork come in?

A team is a group of talented individuals who come together under the leadership of a coach/manager to utilize their unique strengths to accomplish an agreed-upon goal or vision. In baseball this goal is easy to identify—win enough baseball games to get to the World Series. In other settings the goals may be different, but the concept is the same.

Teamwork is not "group think" or as they like to say in higher education, "shared governance." Team members make decisions within their sphere of responsibility and influence. For example, the short stop makes the decision whether it would be better to throw to first or try and make the double play at second. That is his area of strength and his decision to make. The manager is not going to second guess or try to override that decision. Likewise, the second baseman doesn't get together with his fellow infielders and suddenly decide it is time to replace the pitcher—that's the manager's call, never theirs.

So here's the deal; leaders need teams of talented followers to accomplish their goals and vision. Talented followers need leaders to see the bigger picture and make decisions so they can focus on their strengths, which will benefit the entire team over time.

ACTIVITY FOR THE DAY

Reflect on your team today. Do you have the right people in the right positions? Do they know what they are playing for? Do they know that you see the big picture and will make the decisions you need to make to help your team move forward?

_____

_____

_____

_____

_____

_____

_____

_____

_____

_____

_____

_____

_____

_____

_____

_____

_____

_____

_____

_____

Avoiding Cringe Moments

As leaders, we are usually the ones who are front and center. We do the public speaking, lead the meetings, and articulate on a regular basis where we are going and why.

Our followers want us to do this. It is an encouragement to them to see us leading in this way. However, there is a danger that comes with public speaking—It can lead to "cringe moments" for our followers. So what exactly is a "cringe moment?" It is that moment when the leader has said something publicly that makes their followers cringe and sink down in their seats. It's not good!

Here are some examples of "cringe moments":

1) **The angry outburst that is out of proportion to the situation**

This usually happens during a question and answer time. The question may be somewhat confrontational or even combative, and the leader's response is extremely angry and over the top. We have all experienced this as followers and participants. It makes us feel very uncomfortable.

2) **Delivering grossly inaccurate or under-prepared information**

When this happens it really undermines the follower's trust in their leader's competence. It also has everyone looking around at each other and whispering, "Did they really just say that?"

3) **Public Blaming**

If you want to destroy morale immediately, start blaming people about failures, wrong actions or anything else in public. Remember the old adage, "praise in public, but criticize in private."

4) **Lying**

This one really should be a "no-brainer", but you would be surprised at how many leaders think they can lie about a situation or product in a public meeting. The problem with this is too many people (your followers) know the truth. Lying is a critical wound to a leader's character.

5) **Inappropriate humor or sarcasm**

Humor is a doubled-edged sword. It is either funny or it's not. Is it still funny if it is at someone else's expense, especially, if that person is sitting in the audience? Does the humor flirt with someone's weakness? If the answer is yes, then you can call that inappropriate humor. Don't do it. It demeans your followers. Sarcasm is similar because your followers are not certain if you mean it and that creates a question mark about how they perceive your feelings about them.

6) **Taking credit for someone else's work when you did not contribute anything**

This is a sure way to NOT inspire trust from your followers. This will make for non-stop water cooler discussion regarding whomever's work was slighted. Always give credit to others, even when you did a lot of the work. Your followers will smile instead of cringe.

It is not hard to see why avoiding these types of cringe moments is important for leaders; it damages the one thing that all leaders need from their followers—trust.

Public speaking is not a private conversation; it is public and open to broad interpretation. It is an opportunity to deepen trust, not endanger it.

Will you have a "cringe moment?" YES! We all do, but you want to keep them to a minimum. Be certain to go to your followers and tell them that you shouldn't have said what you said. Remember, your followers are forgiving and they want to defend you to others. But, if you create too many "cringe moments", they will find it much harder to continue to trust you and will be less willing to do so in the future. In their eyes you will have become a "loose cannon", which creates uncertainty for them.

ACTIVITY FOR THE DAY

Have you ever experienced a "cringe moment" as a follower? How did it make you feel? Did it change your perception of the person you were listening to? Have you committed a "cringe moment?" Which category did it fall into?

_____

_____

_____

_____

_____

_____

_____

_____

_____

_____

_____

_____

_____

_____

_____

_____

_____

_____

_____

Nothing Stays The Same

I know a lot of old sayings, so here is another one to add to your list: "The only thing that doesn't change is that everything changes."

Leaders have to ask themselves these questions, "How comfortable am I with change?" "Do I embrace it, ignore it, or try to resist it?" "Is all change good? Is all change bad? How do I discern the difference?"

The simplest definition of change is "to make something different from what it was." It can mean something as simple as changing the color of your hair or a more drastic change in how you look by having cosmetic surgery. It can mean changing the location of where you live or changing jobs. Change happens every day in our personal lives from choosing the type of cereal we eat in the morning to changing the type of shoes we wear. Because we live in a world of constant change most of us try to stake out little areas where we will resist change—we simply want it to stay the same. For me, it used to be my study. I did not want anyone moving or touching anything in my study. I liked it the way it was and didn't want anything to change. It would not surprise me if all of us had areas in our personal lives where we firmly resist change. I understand. It gives us a feeling of peace amidst a bunch of things we can't control.

However, in leading people we cannot hide from change. Many times where we lead people essentially doesn't change, but how we get there does. For me, if I have to re-evaluate where we are going, I call that a strategic change. It will change how my organization looks, thinks, and behaves. If I am looking at how we are going to get there, I call that operational change; is there a better way to get to where we want to go?

In leadership we would prefer that most change be intentional. That is, we initiated the change for a particular reason. Unfortunately, for as many times as we engage in intentional change, there will be just as much unintentional change.

As a leader then, how do I manage change?

1) **Accept change as a normal occurrence**

If your mindset is that change is always happening, then you will not be surprised when it does. Accepting change as a normal part of leading will enable you to create alternative plans and actions more readily and with much less stress. Your followers will also notice that change is not something that disrupts you or throws you into a tailspin. It will make them more open to dealing with change.

2) **Use your intuition and experience to discern good change from bad change**

I wish there was an easier answer to this, but there isn't. All change affects a future that we cannot see, but only imagine or project. This is why intuition must play a part. As we discussed earlier, intuition can connect dots that are not subject to empirical analysis. Experience helps us to determine if the change is good or bad because we have seen it before; maybe in a different form but there is something recognizable to us from our experience.

When you put these things together (intuition and experience) I believe your batting average will be pretty high!

3) **Communicate intentional change with your followers often**

Remember, this is change that you have initiated. Your followers need to know! The more strategic the change, the more you will need to communicate why. Strategic changes affect where we told our followers we were going. It relates to our vision and is one of the reasons they are following us. So, if you alter that you had better be certain that your followers understand why.

4) **Apprise your followers of unintentional changes and that you are dealing with it**

There will always be changes that we cannot anticipate that will affect our followers. You do not have to have an immediate solution or plan, but you do need to let them know that you are aware of the change and that it has affected them. Assure them that you will tell them in a timely manner when you have come up with a plan to deal with the unintentional change.

5) **Always ask yourself, "Am I being pulled by the change or am I pushing the change?"**

This is a good reflective question to ask ourselves as leaders. The truth is that change sometimes pulls us and sometimes we push it. The important thing is to know the difference! We are always more comfortable if we are pushing the change, because we think that what we are changing will be for the better. When we are being pulled by change it usually puts us in a "catch up" mode that feels uncomfortable. When we are unable initiate the change, there is always a lingering uncertainty that the outcome may not be good. So, know which is which and deal with it accordingly!

ACTIVITY FOR THE DAY

List three times that you pushed change in the last three months. How did you communicate with you followers?

List three times that you were pulled by change in the last three months. How did you handle it? How did you communicate to your followers?

_____

_____

_____

_____

_____

_____

_____

_____

_____

_____

_____

_____

_____

_____

_____

_____

_____

_____

Crisis Can Be A Good Thing

It should not surprise you that we are following up our day on dealing with change by talking about crisis. The two often go hand in hand, and many times one causes the other in organizations.

There are different types of crises: natural disaster crisis, personal crisis and organizational crisis. We will only deal with organizational crisis here and how leaders and followers respond to it.

I would guess when you hear the word crisis that your first reaction is that something bad has happened. Well . . . you would be right. The word means that something has happened that will create a struggle, difficulty or trouble. The word also implies that an important decision will need to be made quickly. Crises are a key time that your followers will look to you and expect you to make a decision that will relieve the situation. They will want you to "make it better." Needless to say, this expectation creates stress and tension for the leader.

I have been through it many times and know how it feels. I spent many years walking into organizations that were in crisis. In fact, the crisis was severe enough that they needed outside leadership, someone like me, to come in and address the issues. In every instance I could feel the expectations of the followers—fix the problem!

When faced with a crisis, it's very easy for a leader to become paralyzed about making a decision. Why? It is really very simple. In a crisis you are not afforded the luxury of making a wrong decision. Crises demand the right decision quickly. If a leader begins to worry too much about making a wrong decision, they can become "decision paralyzed." One thing that has helped me avoid decision paralysis through the years is that I have come to recognize that a crisis can be a good thing. Why can I say this? Well, crises always creates some level of organizational pain, and if the pain is intense enough it creates an opportunity for positive change that might not have been possible without the crisis. Leaders who understand this can use a crisis to strengthen an organization and its followers rather than letting the crisis cripple them.

Here are some thoughts to help you view a crisis as a good thing:

1) Organizations seldom embrace change without some level of crisis/pain
2) Crisis creates an opportunity for growth
3) Crisis can deepen the trust that followers have in their leader
4) Crisis will sharpen your decision making as a leader

Here are the most common things that I have seen through the years that lead to organizational crisis:

1) The untimely death or sudden departure of a trusted leader
2) Scandal
3) A series of disastrous business decisions
4) Personnel upheaval/unrest/rebellion

5) Inability to adapt to a changing marketplace

As a leader you will face a crisis at some point; how you view it will make a tremendous difference in how you handle it as well as how your followers will respond to your decisions.

ACTIVITY FOR THE DAY

Reflect on the last time you went through an organizational crisis. How did you react? Do you think leadership responded well or poorly? Why?

To Meet Or Not To Meet?

Let's face it, none of us really like meetings. But, as long as there are leaders and followers there is a need to meet from time to time. So when we call meetings, let's make the most of it.

First, let's talk about why we don't like meetings. Here's a list of some of the most common comments I have heard from followers:

1) A total waste of time
2) Nothing ever gets accomplished or decided
3) Wrong people in the meeting
4) Too many people in the meeting
5) No purpose/agenda to the meeting
6) I have better things to do
7) I don't need to hear the boss talk for an hour about nothing

Do any of these sound familiar to you? I bet you could add one or two of your own! The biggest contributors to these types of negative feelings are the weekly staff meetings; monthly management meetings; etc. These are the meetings where we meet many times just to meet. These are the meetings where agendas are static and repetitive; decisions are not made; new information that may be helpful is not shared in a meaningful way; and last of all, those in attendance do not leave informed or inspired. So, what's the point? I think it is a misconception that just to meet is good leadership. Those who think that could not be more wrong.

When leaders meet with a group of followers (aka, a meeting) there should always be a purpose and inspiration. Remember, you are leading them somewhere, so never miss an opportunity to remind them of where you are going and why this particular meeting is important to that goal. The less you call meetings, the more significant they will appear to your followers. What does that say for the weekly staff meetings?—not very much!

So, as a leader, how do you know when to meet or not to meet? Here are some questions that you should always ask yourself before calling a meeting:

1) Do you have a decision/course of action to communicate?
2) Do you need to bring different parties on board to accomplish a common goal?
3) Do you need to communicate new information that will have an impact on your followers?
4) Do you need to coordinate certain actions/activities with your followers?
5) Do you need to remind your followers how smaller goals link to greater goals?

If you cannot say "yes" to one of these five questions, then you do not need a meeting. If you do need a meeting then be certain to do the following when you lead the meeting:

1) Have a clear, short agenda that is communicated ahead of time to those attending
2) Do your best to have the meeting not go over one hour
3) Don't ramble; don't let others ramble; stay on task

4) If others have a part to play in a meeting, make it clear to them in advance of the meeting
5) Always close by tying in the specifics of the meeting with the greater vision (never miss an opportunity to inspire your followers)

If you do these things, your followers will develop a different attitude about meetings. They will also start to emulate you when they conduct meetings.

ACTIVITY FOR THE DAY

Next time you are in a meeting write down your observations of how the meeting was conducted; each individual's attitude during the meeting, and did the meeting answer any of the five questions posed above.

_____

_____

_____

_____

_____

_____

_____

_____

_____

_____

_____

_____

_____

_____

_____

_____

_____

_____

_____

Sometimes You Just Have To Play Hardball

Several years ago I led a turn-around for an organization that was in significant crisis. This meant that I had to make many tough decisions and have several confrontations with stakeholders and followers. The turn-around took almost two years and ended on a successful note. Toward the end of my time with this organization a senior administrator came to my office to say thank you and give me a gift to commemorate my time spent in helping the organization. When I opened the gift it was a baseball carved out of rock with an inscription that read "Sometimes you just have to play hardball."

One of the toughest things for a leader to know is when to "play hardball." As you know by now, I like baseball and have a tendency to use baseball analogies. There are two types of baseball that are very popular: softball and hardball. In softball the baseball is larger and a little softer; the other is smaller and harder; thus, the phrase "hard ball". Professional baseball is played with the smaller, harder ball. Baseball players will tell you that it is no fun to be hit by a hard ball; it hurts! That's why baseball players wear helmets when they bat and gloves on their hands to field and catch. Have you seen all the gear that catcher's wear to protect themselves from foul balls? You have to stay alert and "on your toes". Playing hardball can hurt!

Do you see where I'm going with this? In leadership, playing hardball means that you are willing to make tough decisions and confront individuals and groups. Many times that may mean that you are taking a stand from which you cannot retreat. All leaders, at one time or another, have to play hardball. The challenge is to discern when you need to play hardball.

Playing leadership hardball always has certain risks. It means you're putting yourself in a win/lose scenario. It means that you could alienate some followers for good. It means that you are convinced that your decision or confrontation is the best way or only way to reach the goal. Here are some questions I ask myself before I decide to play leadership hardball:

1) Is this something that I am "willing to bleed for?" By this I mean, am I willing to deal with any backlash, negativity, or adverse results that come from my decision or confrontation?
2) Do I see that this current obstacle can only be dealt with by direct confrontation?
3) If I do not make this hard decision will I still be able to reach the goal I promised to my followers?

I am certain that there are other questions you can ask yourself, but these three have helped me decide when I needed to play leadership hardball. Remember, it always carries the possibility of someone getting hurt. It is one of the prices we pay to be the leader. One of the reasons our followers trust us is that when the times comes, we are willing to and know when to play leadership hardball.

ACTIVITY FOR THE DAY

Can you remember a time that you had to play leadership hardball? What were your reasons? Did you win or lose? Was it worth it?

_____

_____

_____

_____

_____

_____

_____

_____

_____

_____

_____

_____

_____

_____

_____

_____

_____

_____

_____

_____

Managing People
Is An Art Form

You will recall from the introduction (you did read the introduction, right?) that I made the statement that "all leaders manage, but not all managers lead." An important part of leading is the art of managing people. I call it an art because how to manage people cannot be learned from a book; it can only be learned by doing. I can offer suggestions on how I have effectively managed people, but then you have to take that, try it out, and make it you own. That is why it is like art. To learn how to blend colors and get the desired effect on canvas you have to practice. It is the same way with managing people. Each person is like a work of art that demands an artist's insight and experience to shape them into the most productive and motivated followers.

Managing people is not so much about telling them what to do, as it is inspiring, coaching, empowering, developing and motivating them. It is helping them achieve mutually agreed upon goals and feeling supported.

Everyone is unique. I know that I am stating the obvious, but it is a key truth to keep in mind. Since everyone is different, I need to be able to adjust how I manage each follower individually. Over the next few days I will share with you some insights on managing people that I've learned. Much like various paints on an artist's palette, you will have to try them out, mix them and see how well they work for you. I am certain you will create some new colors that will become the right mix for you.

I know some of you will be asking the question, "What if I have never managed people yet?" My answer is that it is much like learning to swim; you'll never learn if you don't jump in the water. Don't be afraid to try. Remember, managing people is the natural outflow of being an effective leader. The key things which are true for leading people are true for managing them:

1) You must establish trust
2) Use your intuition
3) Be direct and decisive
4) Build on people's strengths

Through the years, I have heard many managers say that managing people was the least favorite part of their job. That should not be the attitude of leaders. Managing people should be something we look forward to doing because leaders are nothing without followers. We should want our followers to be developing, inspired and motivated. Remember, leaders lead groups, but we manage individuals. The two are intrinsically connected.

Since managing people is an art form and not a prescribed formula, we as leaders need to understand that managing people will not always turn out as we thought. What motivates one may not motivate another. This is where we mix the paints and keep trying new approaches. People are worth the effort!

ACTIVITY FOR THE DAY

Who, in your experience, is an artist at managing people? What can you glean and learn from them?

How Not To Manage People

As a rule, people like to be successful and they like to please their leaders/managers. But sometimes, we as managers can make that very difficult. I have heard many complaints about certain management styles. I'm going to share the three most mentioned with you today. Yesterday I said that managing people was an art. Well, keeping with that imagery here are three paint colors to never use!

MANAGING BY SUGGESTION

Followers find this style very frustrating because they are never certain what their manager wants. There are never any specific directions, only vague suggestions on what the manager wants done. Why would anyone manage like this? The answer is really quite simple—if you are never direct or specific, then you can never be held responsible if something doesn't go right. It is much easier for you to say to your followers "I didn't say that" or "that isn't what I told you do." Remember that early on in our discussion of what followers love in leaders is being direct and decisive. Managing by suggestion only confuses your followers and they soon realize that their manager is only looking out for themself.

MANAGING BY HOPING

What can I say? This style is even worse than the previous one. Here the manager gives no direction or suggestion, but hopes that all the followers are doing what they should be doing. This manager spends a lot of time making personal conversation with their followers. When asked how things are going this manager will say, "Things are going fine." What they really mean is "I hope things are going fine." The truth is that they really have no idea how things are going. Their followers will tend to like them, but will not respect or trust them to lead them anywhere. They are on their own. Since they know this, there are two things that will happen: 1) productivity and motivation will plummet and, 2) someone will attempt something they shouldn't because there is no one to tell them differently. Anyone who is managing by hoping is in deep trouble and should consider not managing people.

MANAGING BY RE-DOING

If you want to demoralize your followers, then manage by re-doing. The style is pretty self explanatory. You give someone an assignment or task; they do it, then you re-do it. It does not matter if it was done well, it was just not done your way! This manager has a hard time trusting anyone but themself. Soon this manager will find that no one is really doing anything because they all know that it will be redone by you.

So, what are some guiding principles that almost all followers want from their managers? It's the same things that they want from their leaders! Be direct and decisive; build on your followers strengths and take responsibility.

ACTIVITY FOR THE DAY

Which of the poor management styles cited above have you encountered the most? How did it make you feel as the follower? Are you stuck in one of these poor management styles? List two things that you can do today to help you improve.

_____

_____

_____

_____

_____

_____

_____

_____

_____

_____

_____

_____

_____

_____

_____

_____

_____

How Can I Help You?

One of the keys to managing people is to help them be successful. Sometimes managers forget a very important point; we cannot get anything done without the people following us being successful. I have discovered over the years that a very simple question goes a long way in helping other people succeed. It is, "How can I help you?"

I believe this one question is fundamental to good leadership and good management. It can be asked of every one of your followers regardless of their position or task. It conveys that you, as the leader/manager, care about their success.

It is easy to get caught up in leading the group and forgetting that groups are made up of individuals. By reaching out and asking individual followers the question, "How can I help you?" you build a bridge between the individual and the group. Also, as leaders, we sometimes forget that by our very position we can help get things done for our followers that would be difficult for them to accomplish.

Let me give you an example of this. I had a follower that had been working very hard on a particular project. I could see that they appeared stressed, so I stopped by and asked how things were going. They replied, "Fine." (This is a common response of followers to leaders!) I took it one step further, "Is there anything I can do to help?" The follower paused for a moment and said, "Well, there is one thing that I could use help on; I cannot get a meeting with the key decision maker to move forward on this project." When they told me who it was I said, "No problem, I will take care of that for you." You should have seen the look of relief on their face. It turned out that the key decision maker was someone I knew very well. They took my call immediately (because of my position) and the situation was resolved quickly. By asking that one question it helped my follower be successful. It made them feel supported and moved the project along which was important to our goals.

I could cite many similar situations, but I think you see my point. Leaders/managers not only lead their followers, but they also serve their followers by giving them the help they need at key times. Because of our position as leaders our followers will not usually come ask us for help. We have to take the first step and make the effort to ask.

It is a key question that should be part of your palette as you develop the art of managing people.

ACTIVITY FOR THE DAY

When was the last time a leader/manager asked you, "How can I help you?" When was the last time you asked one of your followers that question? Ask three of your followers this week, "How can I help you?"

_____

_____

_____

_____

_____

_____

_____

_____

_____

_____

_____

_____

_____

_____

_____

_____

_____

_____

_____

_____

_____

The Triangle Of Managing People: Fair

As I have developed my own art of managing people three keys words have emerged that I find essential to managing the vast majority of people who have been willing to follow me. They are FAIR, FRIENDLY and FIRM. I try to envision them as the points on a triangle.

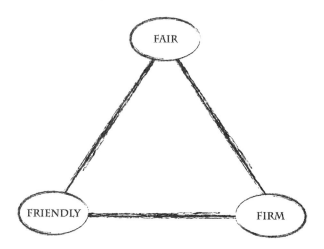

The important thing to know is that my triangle spins, so that at any given time any one of the three words could be at the top of the triangle. Why is it important that my triangle spins? Because each of these words have equal value and are in constant tension with each other. When I am managing people, I am constantly engaging one of these three words depending on the person and the situation. I like to think of these three words as my primary paint colors in mastering the art of managing people. They are to me as red, yellow and blue are to the artist. All other colors come from these three primary colors. So, everything I do in managing people flows from being fair, friendly and firm.

Today we are going to deal with being fair. We have all heard the phrase, "That's not fair!" What does it mean when one of our followers says that? I have learned that it usually means that someone feels they are not being treated equally or someone else is being shown favoritism. When I think of the word fair, I think of being consistent. My followers expect me to behave in a consistent manner toward everyone. It means that I apply the rules and expectations equally to all my followers. It means that I deliver praise and critique equally. This creates a consistency in my management style that my followers can trust. It doesn't mean that they agree with me, but they have come to understand that there is a consistent fairness in my dealings with them. It takes work to be fair because the reality is that leaders/managers don't always feel the same about each of their followers. We like some better than others; we dislike some more than others. Hey, that doesn't sound fair! It's not! That's why it takes work.

If you work at being consistent in your expectations, praise, critiques, and attitude, your followers will perceive you as being fair.

One last thought on being fair—we all know that life isn't fair; but that does not mean that we shouldn't try!

ACTIVITY FOR THE DAY

How would your followers rate you on the fairness scale, 1 being excellent, 5 being poor?

Who is the fairest leader/manager you have followed? Why do you feel this way about him or her?

_____

_____

_____

_____

_____

_____

_____

_____

_____

_____

_____

_____

_____

_____

_____

_____

_____

_____

The Triangle Of Managing People: Friendly

Today we will talk about the second point of the triangle; being friendly.

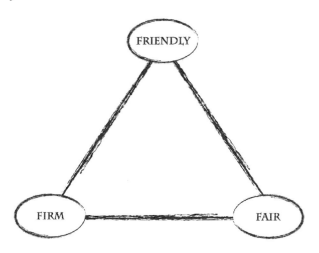

You would be surprised how difficult this is for leaders/ managers. This is because being friendly is not equal to being friends. Let me say it a different way—being friendly does not mean that you are friends or buddies with your followers. Being friendly also means that you are not too distant in your relationships with your followers. Perhaps now you can see why being friendly is difficult to do.

If you become too friendly or become buddies with your followers it can give the appearance to others of you being what? Unfair! If you are too distant, then people think you don't care. So being friendly is like walking a fence; it's easy to fall off on either side.

My dad is a great example of a leader who mastered the art of being friendly. For many years he led a large company. Sometimes, as a youth, I had the opportunity to visit his facilities with him. There were two things I noticed that have remained with me to this day and have shaped how I relate to my followers. The first is that my dad would walk up and say hello to people regardless of their position. It didn't matter if it was the janitor, tradesman, salesperson or administrative personnel. He knew their names, and many times something about their families or interests. Keep in mind this was a big company! The second thing I noticed is that everyone, regardless of their position felt comfortable in calling my dad by his nickname, which was "Rich", being short for Richardson.

My dad didn't socialize with his followers, but they knew he cared. He had mastered the art of being friendly. For a leader, being friendly means that we remember people's names and that we show a genuine interest in them. It also means that we allow them to relate to us on a more informal basis. Doing this will not jeopardize our position as leader. Remember, followers want to follow us, but they also want to feel that we are approachable and that we are interested in them. Who doesn't want to feel that way?

Most of us will have a tendency toward being either too friendly or too distant. The key to improving in this area is to know where your tendency is. You can then begin to nudge yourself toward better balance.

ACTIVITY FOR THE DAY

Write down the name of one person you know who has mastered the art of being friendly. What can you learn from that person?

_____

_____

_____

_____

_____

_____

_____

_____

_____

_____

_____

_____

_____

_____

_____

_____

_____

_____

_____

The Triangle Of Managing People: Firm

The third point of our managing people triangle is being firm.

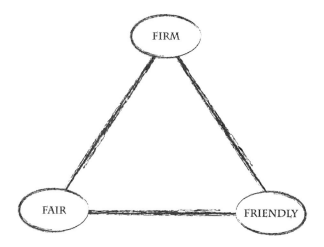

This means when you say something, mean it. When you make a decision, stick with it. If you have asked someone to do something, make certain it happens.

What it does NOT mean is being bossy or unfriendly. This concept of firmness is very closely aligned with being direct and decisive, but it adds the layer that we can call accountability in our followers. Our followers want us, as leaders, to take responsibility. In the same way they also want us to hold them accountable; to adhere to the standard we have set. Followers want us to be firm. It confirms in their mind a sense of fairness, especially if we apply our firmness evenly.

Firmness has to go hand in hand with being friendly. There is an art to being firm, but not nasty or belittling. It's being able to state what needs to be said, while still retaining respect for people and a genuine interest in their success. I have stated this before, but it bears repeating: people may not agree with your decisions, but if those decisions are made in a manner of fairness, friendliness and firmness, they will respect and trust you. And, we now know that if they trust you, they will follow you.

Being firm conveys a sense of confidence in our followers. It says to them that we are not "wishy-washy." It tells them that we will not change our mind based on the next person who comes and complains to us. There is a sense that our decisions are measured and well thought-out. All of this is conveyed when our followers sense firmness in how we manage.

So now, how do we meld the three points of the triangle together? Let me give you some points that will help you develop the ability to incorporate them in your art of managing people.

1) Fair—friendly—firm overlap all the time (one does not outweigh the other)
2) They are always in tension with each other
3) One will usually take the lead in a given situation (what does the follower need most in a given instance?)
4) It takes intention and work to keep them in balance
5) Trust your intuition to help blend them correctly for each person

You are probably saying to yourself right now that being fair, friendly and firm is not that easy! But I said that managing people was an art. Fair, friendly and firm are your three primary colors to create new colors that will help you effectively manage people, and at the same time enjoy doing it. The result of your art is that people will enjoy what they do, they will succeed and feel part of a greater goal. The result is well worth it!

ACTIVITY FOR THE DAY

Do you know someone who has mastered the art of being firm? Are they also fair and friendly? If you are currently managing people, ask yourself if you are balancing being fair, friendly and firm today? Your answer will reveal a lot to you.

_____

_____

_____

_____

_____

_____

_____

_____

_____

_____

_____

_____

_____

_____

_____

_____

_____

_____

A Final Leadership Thought

First, let me thank you for taking these 30 days to become a better leader. It takes commitment to stick with something for 30 days. I'm certain that one or more of these concepts will become a part of your leadership style.

Now, what is my final leadership thought? Here it is, and I think it will surprise you—leaders do not pay that much attention to other leaders. You would think that leaders like to learn from other leaders, discuss best practices—not really! Oh, don't misunderstand me. Leaders like to get together and socialize and talk about successes and new ventures, but very seldom are they looking for advice or insight. It is one of the quirks of being a leader.

Why is that the case? Strong leaders possess self confidence and a certain level of independent purpose. In other words, they trust their own judgment and direction. They don't care what others may think; they know where they want to go, and have a plan on how to get there. Does that sound a little egotistical to you? It is, because it takes a strong ego to lead. I mean this in a positive way. If I do not believe that I can lead my followers somewhere and that my vision for what we are doing is meaningful, then I will not be able to lead effectively. This ego strength comes out in our charisma as leaders. It is part of what draws people to us who want to follow us. This type of healthy, strong ego should never be confused with the idea of being conceited.

Why did I save this thought for the last day? We have spent a good deal of our time on why people follow you and how to effectively lead and manage them. On this last day I wanted to share something important for you alone as the leader. Here it is:

1) Trust yourself; if you don't, others won't
2) Embrace your own ego strength—having a strong ego is not a bad thing
3) Other leaders are not better than you, just different from you

ACTIVITY FOR THE DAY

Write down the three concepts that had the most impact on you from this book. Write down how you think they will change you as a leader.

_____

_____

_____

_____

_____

_____

_____

_____

_____

_____

_____

_____

_____

_____

_____

_____

_____

_____

_____

_____

Acknowledgements

Remember the saying, "It takes a village to raise a child?" The same can be said for writing a book.

It took many years of learning and the experience that came with it, as well as the help of many people to produce an insightful book on leadership.

I would like to thank Janice Cole, my executive assistant and "work wife," Stephanie Richardson, my real-life wife and Megan Richardson, my daughter, for their patience in editing and re-editing each phase of this book.

I would also like to thank my good friends, Sandra Jimenez, Jeff Wojciechowski, Stephen Monteros and Ken Sharrar, who are themselves leaders, for reading the manuscript and providing their individual insights and critiques.

I would like to thank the folks at WestBow Press; especially Stevie Eller, Olivia Allen-Hall and Amanda Parsons, for patiently walking me step by step through the publication process.

And lastly, thanks to the many people whose brains I picked and opinions I asked for; you know who you are! Your input was invaluable in helping me decide to move forward with this book.

I hope you, the reader, have benefited from and enjoyed the experience of looking at being a better leader in this innovative way.

Thank you all.

CPSIA information can be obtained at www.ICGtesting.com
Printed in the USA
LVOW06s0844041113

359647LV00001BB/3/P